D1334963

THE
SOCIAL BITE
COOKBOOK

First published in the UK 2015
Text © Social Bite
Imagery © Freight Books

Co-published with Cargo Publishing

The moral right of Margaret Callaghan to be identified as the author of this work has been asserted by her in accordance with the Copyright, Designs and Patents Act, 1988.

A CIP catalogue reference for this book is available from the British Library.

ISBN 978-1-910741-00-9

Typeset by Freight
Illustrations by Ottavia Pasta
Printed and bound by Bell and Bain, Glasgow

the publisher acknowledges investment from
Creative Scotland toward the publication of this book

THE
SOCIAL BITE
COOKBOOK

Edited by Margaret Callaghan

Illustrations by Ottavia Pasta
Design concept by Kaajal Modi

'Social Bite have set a powerful example on how personal transformation can happen if people on the margins are given a chance. To see the transition of people from homelessness to full time employment is inspirational and it is great to see Scotland leading from the front on this issue through Social Bite.'

Sir Chris Hoy

CONTENTS

SHOWING OFF EASILY

SWEET TREATS

CHEFS' STORIES

FOREWORD

Image by Ilan Ginzburg

I met the founders of Social Bite, Josh and Alice, when they were launching the business 3 years ago. I am delighted to see the growth and success they have achieved since then. As well as serving delicious food, they employ people from homeless backgrounds, donate all the profits to good causes at home and overseas and allow customers to prepay a meal for homeless people. I am sure you will enjoy the recipes shared in this book, as well as the inspirational stories of the formerly homeless people who are now in full time employment and indeed created these dishes. Happy cooking.

Bob Geldof

PREFACE

Thank you for buying the Social Bite cookbook. We started Social Bite in August 2012 with small sandwich shop in Edinburgh and a big dream to bring a "Social Enterprise" business model to the high street. We wanted to compete with all of the big multinational brands, but do so for a social mission, with no individual – including myself – ever getting rich.

Since then, we have made a lot of mistakes, learned a million lessons and built a business that spans every major city in Scotland. We now have a chain of high street sandwich shops in Edinburgh, Glasgow, Aberdeen and Dundee. We sell our wares to thousands of people every day spanning office workers, shoppers, tourists and even builders.

But what makes Social Bite really special is that we exist for a social mission:

- We donate 100% of our profits to charities that we are passionate about.
- We employ 1 in 4 of our workforce from the homeless community.
- And we feed hundreds of homeless people every day with food that our customers have pre-paid for.

Under the guidance of our chef, the recipes in this book were created by people who until recently were living on the streets of Scotland – but are now trained chefs and full time employed. Any profits that we make from this cookbook will go straight back into our work helping the homeless.

We are still learning, we are still making mistakes, but with the support of people like you, I am sure that we will prevail.

Venceremos,

Josh Littlejohn
Co-Founder

FIVE INGREDIENTS

We've all opened up recipe books and closed them again when we've seen a long list of ingredients that you can't find unless you live in London. That's why we thought it would be great to see what we could do with five ingredients. There is a tiny bit of cheating going on as we haven't included oil or seasoning in our five.

2 CHICKEN BREASTS

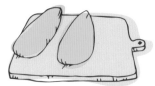

EGG NOODLES

6 NESTS

FRESH GINGER

ABOUT THE SIZE OF YOUR KNUCKLE, THINLY SLICED

CHIPOTLE SAUCE

2 TEASPOONS

OLIVE OIL

2 TABLESPOONS

GREEN CHILLI

1 SMALL, DESEEDED & CHOPPED

SPICY CHICKEN NOODLES

01

SERVES 2

1. Pre-heat your oven to 180 degrees.

2. Cook your noodles in boiling water for about 4–6 minutes. Then run under cold water, let them drain and set aside.

3. Season your chicken breasts with a pinch of salt and pepper. Heat 2 tablespoons of olive oil on a medium heat and cook the chicken for 2 minutes on each side then transfer to an oven dish. Put in the oven and cook for about 12–15 minutes. Test with a sharp knife to make sure it's cooked through. If the chicken is pink inside, return to the oven and cook for a further 4–5 minutes until cooked through.

4. Place a wok or frying pan on a very low heat and add 2 teaspoons of olive oil. Once it's warmed, add the ginger and chilli and cook for about 2 minutes.

5. Add the chipotle sauce to the pan and cook for another minute, then add the noodles. Mix thoroughly and serve with the chicken.

VEGGIE SPINACH AND BABY POTATOES

BABY POTATOES

400 GRAMS

RED ONION

1 LARGE, SLICED

GARLIC

2 CLOVES, MINCED OR CRUSHED

CHESTNUT MUSHROOMS

200 GRAMS, SLICED

OLIVE OIL

3 TABLESPOONS

SPINACH

250 GRAMS

VEGGIE SPINACH AND BABY POTATOES

02

🍲 SERVES 2

"This dish is very easy to make and very tasty, and it's full of nutrients such as iron, potassium, fibre and starch. It can work as a veggie dish for two or as a side for four. Our testers served this on the side with sausages."

1. Bring a pan of water to the boil and then blanch the potatoes for 10–12 minutes, testing they are cooked with a fork (the potatoes should be soft but not breaking up). Drain and set aside.

2. Heat a frying pan on a medium heat, add 3 tablespoons of olive oil then add the potatoes and garlic, tossing them around for 2–4 minutes.

3. Add the rest of the ingredients apart from the spinach and stir everything together for about 3–5 minutes.

4. Finally add the spinach, mixing everything together. Season to taste and serve.

Ian's Story

I was homeless for 14 years. I then started selling The Big Issue, which I did for 7 years outside Sainsbury's on Rose Street in Edinburgh. I built up many regular Big Issue customers, but the income was never steady or reliable and you could be stood in the wind and rain for hours without making much. I am now working full time in Social Bite, making fresh food and serving customers, on the same street I sold the Big Issue on for so long. Many of my old Big Issue customers now recognise me when I serve them in Social Bite and they are really happy that I have found a job. I now live in stable accommodation with my wife and the biggest thing in my life is that I have a job.

Ian Brown

MINUTE STEAKS

2 x 150 GRAMS

2 ONIONS

SLICED

BAGUETTES

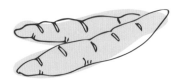

2 SMALL OR 1 LARGE

VEGETABLE OR OLIVE OIL

3 TABLESPOONS

ROCKET OR WATERCRESS

1 HANDFUL

IAN'S STEAK AND CARAMELISED ONION BAGUETTES

⌣ SERVES 2

1. Slice the onions and fry in 2 tablespoons of oil. Keep on a low heat until the onions are browned and sweet to taste (about 10-15 minutes). If you're feeling adventurous you can add a slice of butter and a little brown sugar. Or if you're in a rush, you can use a jar of caramelised onions instead.

2. While the onions are caramelising, season your steaks with a pinch of salt and pepper.

3. Put the steaks in a second frying pan on a high heat and add a tablespoon of oil. Cook the steaks in the pan for one minute each side then put them to one side to rest.

4. Cut the baguette open, add the caramelised onions and rocket or watercress. Cut the steaks in half, add to the baguette, and serve.

STICKY LEMON CHILLI CHICKEN WITH SWEET POTATO WEDGES

04

8 CHICKEN DRUMSTICKS

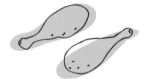

CHILLI FLAKES

1 TEASPOON

HONEY

2 DESSERTSPOONS

2 LARGE SWEET POTATOES

WASHED & CUT INTO WEDGES WITH SKIN ON
(WE RECOMMEND THE WHITE FLESH SWEET POTATO)

CAJUN SPICE OR FAJITA SEASONING

1 TABLESPOON

VEGETABLE OIL

OIL

JUICE OF A LEMON

STICKY LEMON CHILLI CHICKEN WITH SWEET POTATO WEDGES

 SERVES 2

"Tasty and satisfying, particularly if you eat it with your fingers! This is the perfect dish for chilling out with a movie."

1. Using a sharp knife, score the drumsticks at least three times – this will help the flavours to penetrate the chicken flesh. Place the drumsticks in a bowl and sprinkle over the chilli flakes, a pinch of salt and pepper. Drizzle over the lemon juice and the honey. Set aside in the fridge for about an hour to marinade.

2. Once the chicken is marinated, preheat the oven to 180 degrees. Cut the sweet potato into wedges without peeling the skin. Put them in a saucepan covered with cold water and cook them for about 6-8 minutes, then remove from the heat, drain and pat dry with kitchen paper. Season with Cajun seasoning and olive oil. Set aside.

3. Heat 1 tablespoon of vegetable oil on a medium heat. Then pan fry the chicken, turning to stop it from burning. Cook for two minutes on each side.

4. Now place both the chicken drumsticks and wedges into the oven in one dish if that fits. Cook both for 12-15 minutes then serve.

QUESADILLAS WITH RED ONIONS, CHICKEN AND CHORIZO SAUSAGE

CHICKEN

150 GRAMS
CUT INTO SMALL PIECES

1 CHORIZO SAUSAGE

CUT INTO SMALL CUBES

2 PLUM TOMATOES

OLIVE OIL

1 TABLESPOONS

A JAR OF SALSA

8 TORTILLA WRAPS

PLAIN OR WHOLEMEAL

1 SMALL RED ONION

CHOPPED FINELY

CORIANDER

TO GARNISH

CHEDDAR CHEESE

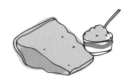

200 GRAMS GRATED

QUESADILLAS WITH RED ONIONS, CHICKEN AND CHORIZO SAUSAGE

05

🍲 SERVES 2

"This is great served with guacamole or an avocado salad."

1. Pre-heat the oven to 180 degrees.

2. Cook onion and chorizo for 2-3 minutes on a medium heat until onion softens.

3. Season the chicken with a pinch of salt and pepper. Add to the pan and cook for about 4-5 minutes, turning regularly.

4. Chop plum tomatoes and add to pan.

5. Arrange 4 tortilla wraps on baking trays. Add the chorizo and chicken mixture, add the grated cheese, and place the remaining 4 tortilla wraps to cover the mixture.

6. Put it in the oven and cook for about 2-3 minutes. Use a fish slice to turn and cook for another 2-3 minutes until the tortilla is golden brown. Then remove, cut into wedges and garnish with a little coriander if desired, with salsa on the side.

JERK PORK CHOPS
WITH ROASTED BUTTERNUT SQUASH

2 PORK CHOPS

1 BUTTERNUT SQUASH

GARLIC

PEELED, SEEDS REMOVED AND
CUT INTO SMALL CUBES

2 CLOVES, CRUSHED

JERK SEASONING

MIXED HERBS

1 TEASPOON

A TEASPOON

JERK PORK CHOPS
WITH ROASTED BUTTERNUT SQUASH

🍲 SERVES 2

1. Marinade the pork with the jerk seasoning. If you like it spicy then you can add more than a teaspoon. We recommend keeping it in the fridge for about 2 hours to marinade, but if you don't have time then you can miss this step.

2. When you're ready to cook it, preheat your oven to 180 degrees.

3. Meanwhile mix the butternut squash in a bowl with the crushed garlic, mixed herbs, seasoning and some vegetable oil.

4. Put both the pork and the butternut squash mixture in the oven, on one tray if you like. Cook for about 15-20 minutes. If the pork is still pink put it back in the oven for another 5 minutes. Serve and enjoy.

BONELESS SALMON

OLIVE OIL

2 TABLESPOONS

TOMATO

1 LARGE, SLICED

8 NEW POTATOES

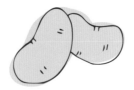

FRESH BASIL

6 LEAVES, ROUGHLY CHOPPED

TOMATO AND BASIL SALMON WITH NEW POTATOES

 SERVES 2

"Healthy, light and delicious."

1. Preheat your oven to 190 degrees.

2. Drizzle some oil on a baking tray. Place the salmon on this, skin side down. Season with a pinch of salt and pepper, top with the tomato slices and drizzle more oil on top of the fish. Bake in the oven for about 15-20 minutes.

3. Meanwhile put the potatoes in cold water and bring to the boil, then turn down and simmer. They should be ready at the same time as the salmon.

4. Drain the potatoes and season well, take the salmon out the oven, add the basil on top of the fish and serve.

LUNCHES TO GO

Sometimes it's good to have a change from a sandwich so we've given you seven different ideas for lunches that can be popped in a plastic container and taken to the office. They all serve two so you can use them for two days, impress your partner, serve them as a side dish at night or multiply up for the whole family.

Once you've made these seven you can easily start to adapt them, using up food that is in your fridge or experimenting by adding other ingredients that you like. Soon you'll be the envy of your workplace! Of course if you really can't be bothered making lunch you can always pop into your nearest Social Bite.

GOAT'S CHEESE AND SPINACH FRITTATA

SPINACH

250 GRAMS

OLIVE OIL

3 TABLESPOONS

GARLIC

2 CLOVES, FINELY CHOPPED

EGGS

5 MEDIUM

GOAT'S CHEESE

75 GRAMS

ONION

HALF A MEDIUM, CHOPPED

MILK

1 TABLESPOON

SALT & PEPPER

TO TASTE

GOAT'S CHEESE AND SPINACH FRITTATA

08

🍲 SERVES A HUNGRY 2

"Frittatas are a great way to use up leftovers and you can really experiment with them. We make them to use up leftover cooked broccoli, mushrooms or potatoes, and maybe add some blue cheese if we happen to have some. Even the most nervous cook among our friends was making frittatas regularly once they'd seen how easy they were."

1. Preheat the oven to 200 degrees.

2. Cook the spinach on a low heat until it's just wilted, which should take two or three minutes. Spinach doesn't need much water to cook so the water remaining from washing should be enough but add a little more if you need to.

3. In a bowl, whisk together the eggs and milk and season with salt and pepper. Set aside.

4. Slowly cook the onions in olive oil in an ovenproof frying pan until translucent, which will take about 4-5 minutes on medium heat. Add the garlic and cook a minute further.

5. Mix the cooked chopped spinach in with the onions and garlic, then pour over the milk and egg mixture. Use a spatula to lift up the spinach mixture along the sides of the pan to let the egg mixture flow underneath. Dot bits of goat cheese over the top of the frittata mixture.

6. When the mixture is about half set, put the whole pan in the oven. Bake for 13-15 minutes, until the frittata is puffy and golden. Remove from oven with oven mitts and let it cool for several minutes.

7. If you're taking it to work then cut a generous slice and put in a box perhaps with some salad. It's so quick and easy to make, it's also nice as a fast dinner or a weekend brunch. You might want to make this hot for Sunday and have the leftovers for Monday lunch at work. From my experience you should be careful to wear oven mitts when you touch the handle. Ouch.

BLUE CHEESE AND WALNUT SALAD

BABY SPINACH

A LARGE HANDFUL

HONEY

1 TABLESPOON

LEMON JUICE

2 TABLESPOONS

BLUE CHEESE

75 GRAMS

1 APPLE

CORED AND CUT
INTO LARGE SLICES

OLIVE OIL

3 TABLESPOONS

CIDER VINEGAR

A TABLESPOON

HANDFUL OF WALNUTS

BLUE CHEESE
AND WALNUT SALAD

09

☕ SERVES 2

1. Toss the apples with 1 tablespoon of lemon juice – this stops them from going brown.

2. Place the spinach in a large bowl; remove the long stems and bruised leaves.

3. Whisk together the remaining lemon juice, olive oil, vinegar, honey, salt, and ground pepper to taste.

4. Toss the spinach with apples and the dressing. Top with cheese and walnuts. If you happen to have grapes in then you could add these too. You can also swap the blue cheese for cheddar if you prefer. Serves two for lunch or a starter, but you could also make up a batch to take to a party.

CHILLI CHICKEN
AVOCADO WRAP

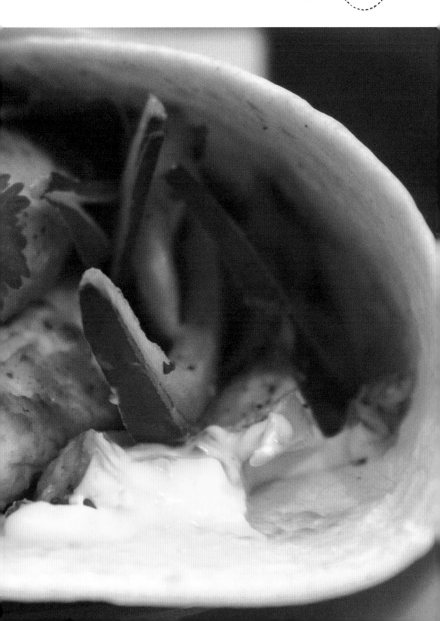

2 TORTILLA WRAPS

1 CHICKEN BREAST

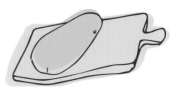

CUT INTO STRIPS

CRÈME FRAÎCHE

2 TEASPOONS

1 RED ONION

THINLY SLICED

1 AVOCADO

THINLY SLICED

OLIVE OIL

2 TABLESPOONS

1 SMALL CHILLI

DESEEDED AND FINELY CHOPPED
(USE LESS IF YOU DON'T LIKE SPICY THINGS)

JUICE OF A LEMON

CHILLI CHICKEN AVOCADO WRAP

 SERVES 2

"This is good when you want to use up leftover roast chicken, and then you don't even have to cook the chicken!"

1. Cut your chicken breast into strips and season with salt and pepper.

2. Place a pan on a medium heat with 2 tablespoons of olive oil, then add your chicken. Cook for about 6-8 minutes then set to one side.

3. Mix the lemon juice, crème fraîche and chillies together. Gently spread the mixture onto the wrap, then add the sliced onion, avocado and chicken. Fold the wrap over and serve.

TIP: TEST IF AN AVOCADO IS RIPE BY HOLDING IN PALM OF HAND AND GENTLY SQUEEZING. DON'T USE YOUR FINGERS AS THIS WILL BRUISE IT.

Joseph's Story

I was put into care when I was five years old, and spent the next ten years in and out of different homes. My little brother and I got separated. Sometimes we'd get to live together, but a lot of the time that wasn't the case and we'd be lucky to see each other at all. I didn't enjoy school. It seemed like I was a liability to everyone around me.

Once I became an adult my life was already messed up, and without a stable home or chance of getting a job I quickly became homeless and eventually found myself selling the Big Issue, and crashing on couches or under a bridge most nights.

I started working for Social Bite three years ago and since then my life has become more and more stable. I started on the dishes at the first Social Bite shop on Rose Street and now I'm working in the central kitchen as a commis chef and am currently being encouraged to work on my management skills so that I can hopefully have the option of a more managerial role one day. I'm also a pretty awesome commis chef now! I live in Livingston just near my work with my buddy Colin who also works for Social Bite and we have a good laugh together.

Joseph Hart

GARLIC

1 CLOVE, CRUSHED

OLIVE OIL

1 TABLESPOONS

ROCKET

150 GRAMS

1 CUCUMBER

CUT INTO SMALL CUBES

FETA CHEESE

100 GRAMS, CRUMBLED

10 CHERRY TOMATOES

CUT INTO HALVES

1 CRUSTY ROLL

TO SERVE

JUICE OF A LEMON

JOSEPH'S FETA, TOMATO, CUCUMBER AND ROCKET SALAD

 SERVES 2

"On a hot summer day this salad tastes very fresh, it's easy to make and very cheap."

1. Assemble the rocket in a large salad bowl, and add the tomatoes and cucumber.

2. Crumble the feta into the bowl and toss the ingredients together.

3. Mix the garlic, lemon juice, olive oil, and a pinch of rock salt together. Drizzle over the salad.

4. Put in a box, take it to work and enjoy it for your lunch with a crusty roll.

INSTANT COUSCOUS

200 GRAMS

DRIED APRICOTS OR SULTANAS OR A MIXTURE

A HANDFUL, CHOPPED

BOILING WATER OR STOCK

250 ML

OLIVE OIL

5 TABLESPOONS

1 RED PEPPER

DICED

BALSAMIC VINEGAR

5 TABLESPOONS

RED ONION

1 SMALL, FINELY SLICED

MINT LEAVES

TO SERVE

CHERRY TOMATOES

150 GRAMS, CUT INTO HALVES

CUCUMBER

1 SMALL, DICED

COUSCOUS IN A HURRY

 SERVES 2

"It's great to make a bowlful of this at the start of the week and use for a few days' lunch. It also makes an easy side dish when you're serving lamb."

1. Place the couscous in a large bowl and pour over the boiling water or stock. Cover the bowl with Clingfilm and set aside for 5 minutes, or until the water is absorbed, then fluff with a fork.

2. Stir the cherry tomatoes, cucumber, pepper, apricots and red onion into the couscous.

3. Make a dressing by placing the oil and balsamic vinegar in a screw-topped jar and shaking well until combined.

4. Season the couscous well with salt and freshly ground black pepper and drizzle over the dressing.

5. Tear up a handful of mint leaves and toss through the salad.

LOW-FAT CREAM CHEESE

100 GRAMS

1 LEMON

FRESH FLAT-LEAF PARSLEY

1 SMALL BUNCH, LEAVES PICKED

SMOKED MACKEREL

200 GRAMS

MACKEREL PÂTÉ ON CRACKERS

 SERVES 2

"It's so easy and yet people are really impressed."

1. Peel the skin off the smoked mackerel and discard. Put the fish in a food processor (a stick blender would also work), breaking it up slightly as you go.

2. Add the cream cheese, the zest and the juice of the lemon, and a few leaves of parsley. Whiz for 20 seconds or so, or until you get a nice creamy pâté. Season to taste and top with the remainder of parsley.

3. Take in a box to work and add some crackers, bread, or vegetable sticks. This can also be served with cucumber or carrot sticks as a healthy starter.

TIP: YOU CAN BUY SMOKED MACKEREL CHEAPLY IN A VACUUM PACK FROM MOST SUPERMARKETS.

BLACK BEAN SALAD

BLACK BEANS

1/2 A TIN, DRAINED
APPROX. 115 GRAMS

SWEET CORN

1/2 A TIN, DRAINED
APPROX. 100 GRAMS

1/2 AVOCADO

CUT INTO CHUNKS

1 SHALLOT

CHOPPED

OLIVE OIL

1/2 TABLESPOONS

2 TOMATOES

CHOPPED

JUICE OF A LIME

JALAPEÑOS

SEVERAL SLICES (FROM A JAR)

CORIANDER

TO GARNISH

BLACK BEAN SALAD

🍲 SERVES 2

1. In a large bowl, gently combine the black beans, corn, shallot, minced jalapeños, chopped tomatoes, lime juice, and olive oil.

2. Gently fold in the chopped avocados. (If you are taking this to work or using over a few days you might want to keep the avocado separate and add it before you eat to prevent it from going brown.)

3. Add salt and pepper and sprinkle with sugar to taste, enough to balance the acidity from the tomatoes and lime juice.

4. Chill before serving, and garnish with coriander.

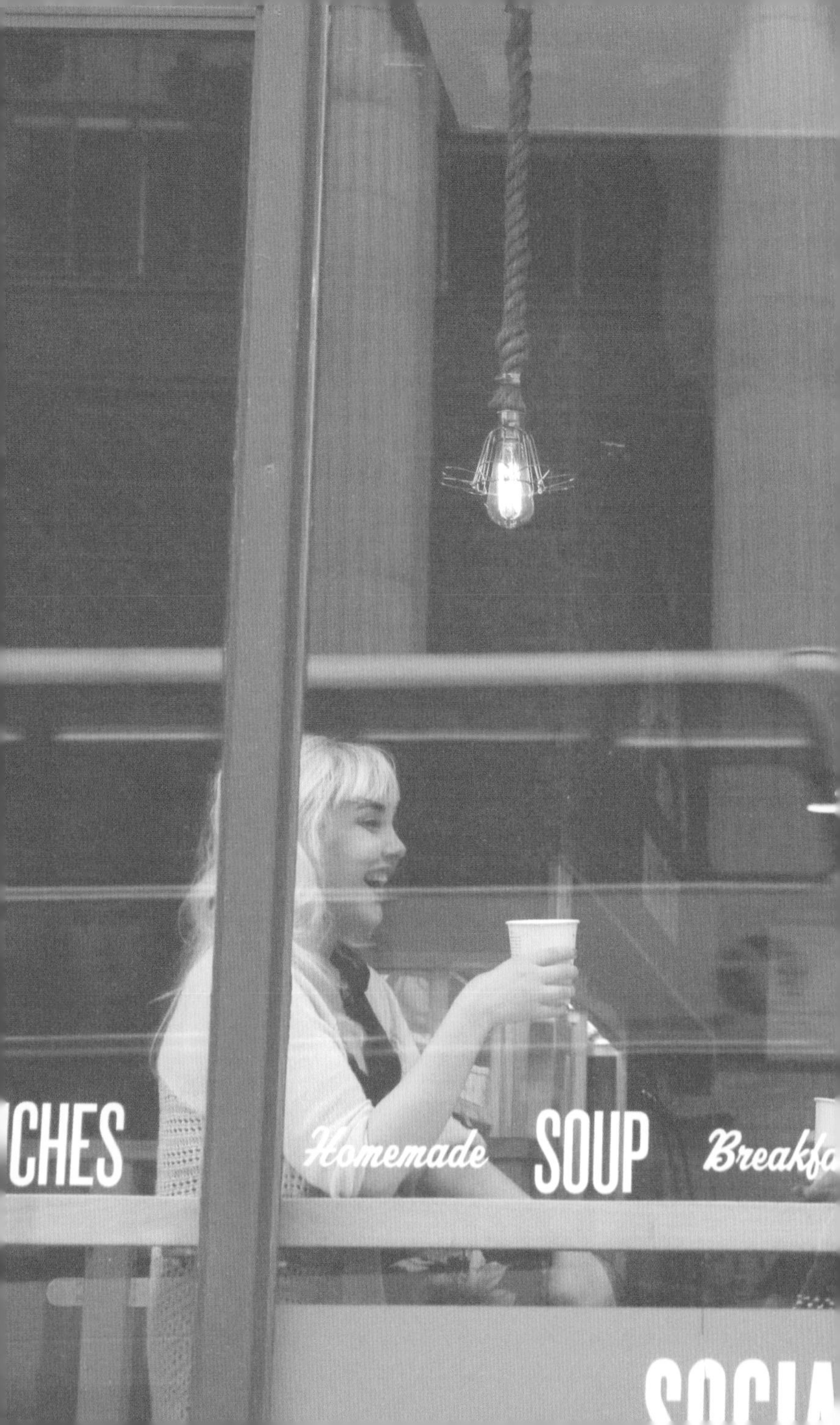
CHES
Homemade
SOUP
Breakfa

AGELS Hot MEALS   Healthy

ONE POT WONDERS

One of the worst things about cooking is being left with a whole pile of washing up. Although of course someone else should really be doing this if you cooked... So we've come up with some One Pot Wonders where everything can be cooked in the one pot for minimum cleaning and maximum taste.

4 CHICKEN THIGHS

TAKE ANY FAT OFF AND
CUT INTO 2CM PIECES

CHILLI FLAKES

2 TEASPOONS

CORN FLOUR

4 TEASPOONS

VEGETABLE OIL

3 TABLESPOONS

FRESH GINGER

1 SMALL PIECE
(THE SIZE OF THE TOP OF YOUR
THUMB) — THINLY SLICED

1 PEPPER

CHOPPED

GARLIC

1 CLOVE CRUSHED

1 CARROT

PEELED AND SLICED

1 FRESH CHILLI

DESEEDED AND
ROUGHLY CHOPPED

CHOPPED TOMATOES

1 TIN

FRESH THYME

3 SPRIGS

MICHAEL'S JAMAICAN CHICKEN STEW

 SERVES 2

1. Rub the chilli flakes with a pinch of salt onto the chicken and put into the fridge for about an hour. This will allow the flavours to infuse the chicken. Now wash your hands very carefully. If you've ever rubbed your eyes or taken out contact lenses after touching chilli you won't ever do it again...

2. Heat two tablespoons of the vegetable oil on a high heat. Meanwhile dust the chicken with the corn flour shaking off any excess. Deep fry for about 3 minutes until golden brown and crispy, then remove and pat with kitchen paper to get rid of excess oil. Wash and dry the pan.

3. Heat one tablespoon of vegetable oil on a medium heat and add all of the vegetables except the tomatoes (yes we know they're a fruit). Cook for about four minutes until the vegetables are soft.

4. Now add the tin of tomatoes and the thyme and some water if you need it. Let it all cook for about fifteen minutes.

5. Finally add the chicken and cook for another ten minutes until everything is warm. Serve with a hunk of bread.

VEGETABLE OIL

2 TABLESPOONS

1 SMALL WHITE ONION

FINELY CHOPPED

GARLIC

1 CLOVE CRUSHED

CHOPPED TOMATOES

400 GRAMS TIN

CHILLI POWDER

1 TEASPOON (ADD MORE IF
YOU LIKE IT MORE SPICY)

VEGETABLE STOCK

2 TABLESPOONS

KIDNEY BEANS

400 GRAMS TIN
DRAINED AND RINSED

HARICOT BEANS

DRAINED AND RINSED

CANNELLINI BEANS

DRAINED AND RINSED

DICED PEPPER

HALF EACH OF A RED,
GREEN AND YELLOW PEPPER

3 BEAN CHILLI

🍲 SERVES 2

1. Heat the oil on a medium heat, then add the onions and garlic and cook for about 3-4 minutes until soft.

2. Mix in the chilli powder, then add the tomatoes and stock and cook for a further 6-8 minutes.

3. Next add all of the beans, mixing gently so that they don't get mushy, and the diced peppers. Cook for ten minutes.

4. Enjoy it hot or cold, with a wrap or with a baked potato, and serve with natural yoghurt if you have some.

STREAKY BACON

6 CHOPPED RASHERS

BUTTER

1 KNOB

PARMESAN CHEESE

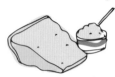

50 GRAMS GRATED

FROZEN PEAS

100 GRAMS

OLIVE OIL

2 TABLESPOONS

1 ONION

FINELY CHOPPED

RISOTTO RICE

300 GRAMS

HOT VEGETABLE STOCK

1 LITRE

QUICK PEA AND HAM RISOTTO

 SERVES 2

"Risotto usually requires adding ingredients slowly and lots of lazy stirring but here we've got a quick version. You can experiment by adding prawns and mint instead of bacon or swapping the bacon for Parma ham or pancetta."

1. Finely chop the onion. Heat 2 tablespoons of olive oil and a knob of butter in a pan, add the onions and fry until lightly browned (about 7 minutes). Add the bacon and fry for a further 5 minutes, until it starts to crisp.

2. Add the rice and stock, and bring to the boil. Stir well then reduce the heat and cook, covered, for 15-20 minutes until the rice is almost tender.

3. Stir in the peas, add a little salt and pepper and cook for a further 3 minutes, until the peas are cooked. Serve sprinkled with freshly grated parmesan and freshly ground black pepper.

Every time it comes to defrosting the fridge there is a bag of frozen peas, which usually gets made into pea and mint soup (boil peas in ham stock, blend, add mint). But this is a great alternative for at least some of the peas!

Sonny's Story

When I was a baby my family were subjected to the traumatic experience of being held hostage in our own home, for several hours one day, and threatened at knife point. After this my mother suffered PTSD and I was placed in care. Although I maintained a great relationship with my mum, life was unsteady for me growing up. I moved around a lot and never found my feet with a career.

Not having regular income made it impossible to have a home and I began stealing things from shops, either food for me or things I could sell on to others to make some quick cash. Eventually I got caught and spent time in jail. The really surprising thing is that this is where I became addicted to heroin. This was a dark and difficult time for me, following the death of my mother, leaving jail with no prospects and a drug addiction I did not have when I went in.

Eventually my partner and I got pregnant and realised we had to change our lives. We got sober with the help of DTTO (Drug Treatment and Testing Order), and I was offered a job with Social Bite. I started just 2 hours a day flyering for the shops, and now I work full time at the central kitchen. I will soon be moving to one of our new Social Bite units inside a cool company called Rockstar Games' office block, which I'm really excited about, and I'm much better.

Sonny

BEEF

300 GRAMS DICED

2 CARROTS

DICED

GRAVY GRANULES

1 TABLESPOON

MUSHROOMS

150 GRAMS

1 ONION

DICED

8 BABY POTATOES

CUT IN HALF

BEEF STOCK

300ML MADE UP FROM
TWO BEEF STOCK CUBES

FRESH THYME

3 SPRIGS

RED WINE

150ML

STEW SONNY MURRAY

 SERVES 2

"Great to come home to on a cold winter's day. You might want to make double and freeze half for one of those days when you're too tired to cook."

1. Soak the beef in the stock overnight or as long as possible in the stew pot.

2. Add all of ingredients except the potatoes to the pot. Cook at a simmer on the stove, on a low heat for forty minutes, adding water if it gets too dry.

3. Add the potatoes and cook another twenty minutes or until the potatoes are ready. How easy was that?

SEAFOOD STEW
ON A BUDGET

2 CELERY STICKS

CHOPPED

CRÈME FRAÎCHE

2 TABLESPOONS
(LOW FAT IF YOU PREFER)

1 GARLIC CLOVE

CRUSHED

1 ONION

CHOPPED

FROZEN SEAFOOD

400 GRAMS OF DEFROSTED
OR READY-MADE SEAFOOD
MIX FROM THE FISH COUNTER

FISH STOCK

300 ML
MADE FROM STOCK CUBES

OLIVE OIL

2 TABLESPOONS

CORN FLOUR

1 TEASPOON

WHITE WINE

175ML (A SMALL GLASS)

DILL OR TARRAGON

FOR GARNISH

SEAFOOD STEW ON A BUDGET

⌣ SERVES 2

"There's something about fish stew that really impresses people because so many people are nervous of cooking fish. This one is quick, easy and healthy. Give it a try."

1. Heat the oil in a large frying pan on a low heat and cook the onion and celery until soft but not coloured, this should take about ten minutes.

2. Add the garlic and cook for another minute. Pour in the wine and simmer on a high heat until most has disappeared.

3. Pour in the stock and cornflour, mix and simmer for five to ten minutes, stirring often until thickened.

4. Season, then add the seafood. Simmer for a few minutes until piping hot, then stir in the crème fraîche.

5. Ladle into two deep bowls. Garnish with dill or tarragon. This is lovely with some garlic bread and the rest of the wine.

PORK

200 GRAMS
CUT INTO 5CM CUBES

1 SWEET POTATO

CUT INTO CHUNKS
USE THE WHITE FLESH POTATOES,
THIS IS GOOD FOR STEWS AS IT CAN
ABSORB MORE LIQUID AND STAY TENDER

1 SMALL CHILLI

DESEEDED AND CHOPPED

PLAIN FLOUR

2 TABLESPOONS

VEGETABLE OIL

2 TABLESPOONS

1 LARGE WHITE ONION

CHOPPED

CHOPPED TOMATOES

400 GRAMS TIN

2 CARROTS

SLICED

HAM STOCK

150ML

2 BAY LEAVES

PORK STEW

🍲 SERVES 2

1. Mix the flour with a pinch of salt then coat the pork in the flour mixture.

2. Heat the oil in a deep pan on a medium heat. Add the pork and cook for about 8-10 minutes until slightly brown.

3. Add the ham stock, carrots, chilli, bay leaves, onions, and chopped tomatoes. Put the lid on and let it cook for about 25-30 minutes.

4. Add the chunks of sweet potato and cook for a further 10-12 minutes. Then it's ready to eat!

CHICKPEAS

400 GRAMS TIN

CAULIFLOWER

HALF A HEAD

1 CARROT

MEDIUM-SIZED, CHOPPED

6 MUSHROOMS

SLICED

½ AN ONION

CHOPPED

SPINACH

LARGE HANDFUL, CHOPPED

GARLIC

3 CLOVES, CHOPPED

2 TOMATOES

DICED

1 RED CHILI PEPPER

DESEEDED AND CHOPPED

VEGETABLE STOCK

200ML

CUMIN

1 TABLESPOON

CURRY POWDER

½ A TEASPOON

TURMERIC

1 TEASPOON

CAYENNE

A DASH

CORIANDER

1 TEASPOON

SALT

½ A TEASPOON

CHICKPEA STEW

 SERVES 2

"This is perfect for persuading carnivores to eat more vegetables – and it covers most of your five a day."

1. Sauté the onions, garlic and chili pepper until soft.

2. Add in the carrots, mushrooms and cauliflower and stir for a few minutes until the vegetables soften slightly.

3. Add the vegetable stock, tomatoes, chickpeas, salt and spices. Cook, covered, for about 10 minutes or until the vegetables are tender. Add more liquid or spices to taste.

4. Toss in the spinach leaves and heat for a few minutes until they are wilted. Serve and be proud of yourself – it's good for you and delicious!

SHOWING OFF EASILY

A hot date, an old friend, an apology? Sometimes in life we want to impress someone without spending hours in the kitchen or days hunting down obscure ingredients. All of these recipes can be found in your local supermarket and made quickly for instant kudos.

CHICKEN WITH MOZZARELLA AND PARMA HAM

Served with Honey Roasted Baby Vegetables

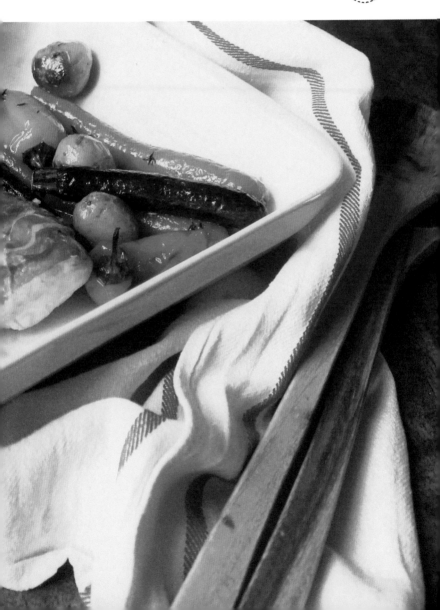

CHICKEN

2 SMALL BREASTS

GARLIC

2 CLOVES CRUSHED

PARMA HAM

4 SLICES
(BACON WORKS IF THAT'S WHAT
YOU HAVE, STREAKY IS BEST)

HONEY

2 TEASPOONS

MIXED BABY VEG

E.G. BABY PARSNIPS,
BABY CARROTS, BABY
POTATOES, BABY LEEKS

MOZZARELLA

1 BALL CUT INTO 4 SLICES

OLIVE OIL

2 TABLESPOONS

FRESH OREGANO

2 SPRINGS

FRESH THYME

4 SPRIGS

CHICKEN WITH MOZZARELLA AND PARMA HAM

Served with Honey Roasted Baby Vegetables

SERVES 2

1. Preheat the oven to 180 degrees.

2. Use a sharp knife to make a pocket in each chicken breast. Stuff the chicken breasts with the sliced mozzarella and sprinkle with the oregano, then gently wrap each breast with two slices of Parma ham and put aside.

3. Cut the potatoes in half and boil for around ten minutes so that they yield to a fork but are not ready.

4. Meanwhile mix the olive oil, pinch of salt, garlic, thyme and honey together.

5. Put the chicken breasts on a large oven tray. Drain the potatoes and add the other vegetables, then toss them together with the flavoured olive oil and add to the oven tray around the chicken in a single layer.

6. Cook in the oven for twenty-five minutes or until the chicken is cooked through. When it's ready, use a sharp knife to cut the chicken into slices at an angle and assemble your roasted veg on the side of the plate and the chicken in the centre. Pour the juice from the pan over the chicken. YUM.

BEEF

320 GRAMS IN STRIPS

8 BABY CORNS

BROCCOLI

HALF HEAD CUT
INTO SMALL PIECES

2 CARROTS

USE A VEG PEELER TO SHAVE

2 SPRING ONIONS

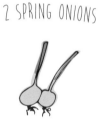

GARLIC

1 CLOVE — CRUSHED

OYSTER SAUCE

2 TABLESPOONS

DARK SOY SAUCE

1 TABLESPOON

VEGETABLE OIL

2 TABLESPOONS

STIR FRY BEEF
Served with Rice or Noodles

⌁ SERVES 2

1. Heat the oil in a wok if you have one, if not in a large frying pan. Add the beef and fry for 3-5 minutes, stirring all the time.

2. Turn the heat down to medium and add the broccoli and baby corn, then after 2 minutes add the rest of the vegetables.

3. Keep tossing the veg and beef then add the soy sauce and oyster sauce and cook for another 2 minutes.

4. Serve with rice or quick cook noodles. Another masterpiece in fifteen minutes.

Colin's Story

I spent 16 years of my life living on a bus and travelling around Britain. It was a fun time for me, but when the hang over wore off and I realised I was 36 with no home or job to come back to real life with; I was in a bit of trouble. I moved in with a girlfriend and made ends meet however I could, but I became homeless when I fell out with my girlfriend 5 years ago. I lived on the streets with a pet dog and tried to crash on couches and in hostels when I could.

Eventually I started selling the Big Issue on street corners. However 2 years ago I heard about Social Bite and managed to get a job there being a kitchen porter, a few hours a day, with the promise of full time hours as soon as a position was available. True to their word I'm now working full time in the central kitchen where I make all of the panini and focaccia breads and live with my mate Joe who works there too. I'm also now in a great relationship with my girlfriend Sam who stays in Dundee, where I'm from, and once Social Bite opens a store in Dundee in the next year or two, I will get to move up there to be with her full time and work in the shop.

Colin

2 MACKEREL FILLETS

RED PESTO SAUCE

2 TEASPOONS

8 BABY POTATOES

CUT IN HALF

FROZEN PEAS

150 GRAMS

8 CHERRY TOMATOES

CUT IN HALF

LEMON WEDGES

COLIN'S ROAST MACKEREL WITH RED PESTO
Served with Baby Potatoes and Peas

 SERVES 2

"Mackerel is a really under rated fish but one of the most economical that you can eat in the UK especially during the summer months. It's also one of the highly recommended oily fish for a healthy diet as it's rich in essential oil, vitamins and minerals."

1. Place your mackerel fillets on a chopping board, skin side up. Use a sharp knife to score (cut) the skin 3 times but don't cut too deeply or the fish will fall apart. Spread a teaspoon of the red pesto sauce on each fillet and leave in the fridge for at least an hour.

2. When you're ready to eat, preheat your oven to 180 degrees.

3. Cut the potatoes in half and put in a pan of cold water, making sure the water covers the potatoes. Add a pinch of salt, bring to the boil, then lower the heat to a simmer and cook for around 10-12 minutes, testing with a fork to make sure they're ready.

4. Meanwhile place the fish on a tray and cook in the oven for 8-10 minutes.

5. Boil the peas for about 3 minutes, then drain.

6. Heat up a tablespoon of olive oil in a pan and add the peas and cherry tomatoes and cook for 3 minutes. Season with salt and pepper. Then plate up and garnish with lemon. A whole show off dinner in fifteen minutes (minus marinating)!

VEGETABLE KEBAB
Served with Couscous and Yoghurt Dressing

For the Skewers

2 PEPPERS

RED OR YELLOW
CUT INTO LARGE CHUNKS

1 LARGE RED ONION

CUT INTO THICK WEDGES

6 CHESTNUT MUSHROOMS

THICKLY SLICED

1 SMALL COURGETTE

THICKLY SLICED

OLIVE OIL

2 TABLESPOONS

1/2 A LEMON

GARLIC

1 CLOVE

MIXED HERBS

VEGETABLE KEBAB

Served with Couscous and Yoghurt Dressing

 SERVES 2

For the Skewers

1. Preheat your oven to 180 and boil a kettle of water. TIP: Soak your skewers in water. This will prevent them burning when you put them in the oven or barbecue.

2. Toss the peppers, courgettes, onions and mushrooms in a dressing made of 2 tablespoons of olive oil, a crushed clove of garlic, salt, pepper, mixed herbs and a squeeze of lemon.

3. Thread the peppers, onions, courgettes and mushrooms onto the skewers. Put on a oven tray and put in the hot oven. Cook for 10-12 minutes.

COUSCOUS

100 GRAMS

GARLIC

1 CLOVE CRUSHED

10 OLIVES

STONED AND ROUGHLY CHOPPED

VEGETABLE STOCK

200ML MADE WITH A
VEGETABLE STOCK CUBE

OLIVE OIL

4 TABLESPOONS

1/2 A RED ONION

FINELY DICED

For the Couscous

1. Heat 4 tablespoons of oil in a pan on a low heat. Add the diced onions, olives and crushed garlic.

2. Once they have softened add half of the stock, and then once the water is boiling mix well and add the couscous. This will allow the couscous to incorporate all the flavours.

3. Turn the heat down to very low and gently add the remainder of the stock and stir the couscous. Then put a lid on the pot and turn the heat off. The couscous will incorporate the water from the stock.

NATURAL YOGHURT

200ML

FRESH MINT

4 SPRIGS

CORIANDER

FOR GARNISH

For the Dressing

1. Put the yoghurt in a bowl and add the chopped mint.

2. Now serve the couscous with the skewers on top and the dressing drizzled across both. Garnish with chopped coriander.

PENNE PASTA

300 GRAMS

1 HEAD OF BROCCOLI

CUT INTO SMALL PIECES

SMOKED BACON

4 SLICES ROUGHLY CHOPPED

2 EGG YOLKS

WHISKED

1 SHALLOT

FINELY DICED

PARMESAN CHEESE

50 GRAMS GRATED

DOUBLE CREAM

1 TABLESPOON

OLIVE OIL

1 TABLESPOON

GARLIC

1 CLOVE CRUSHED

JOHNNY'S PASTA CARBONARA

 SERVES 2

"Everyone has their different version of this Italian classic. Here's Johnny's version – it's a good one!"

1. Cook the pasta in boiling water with a pinch of salt for 10 minutes. Remove from the heat and drain, but keep the water. Put the cooked pasta to one side.

2. Use the same water to cook the broccoli for three minutes, then drain and run under cold water. This will help it retain its colour and freshness.

3. Heat the oil in a large frying pan. Add the bacon and shallots and cook for 3-4 minutes. Add the garlic and cook for a further 2 minutes, then add the cream and let it simmer for 2-4 minutes on a low heat.

4. Add half of the Parmesan cheese and the yolks, then mix really well.

5. Finally, add in the pasta and the broccoli, stir well, serve onto plates and sprinkle with the rest of the cheese.

2 CHICKEN BREASTS

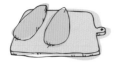

CUT INTO CUBES

BUTTER

20 GRAMS

DOUBLE CREAM

150ML

GARLIC

6 CLOVES CRUSHED

CHESTNUT MUSHROOMS

50 GRAMS, SLICED

1 LEEK

FINELY CHOPPED

VEGETABLE OIL

1 TABLESPOON

CHICKEN STOCK

1 CUBE, CRUMBLED

WHITE WINE

150ML

CREAMY GARLIC CHICKEN

⌂ SERVES 2

1. Heat 1 tablespoon of vegetable oil in a pan, then add the chicken and brown.

2. Next add the butter, chopped leeks, mushrooms and garlic. Let it cook for about 4-5 minutes until soft, then add the wine and let it simmer for about 3-5 minutes. This will allow the alcohol to evaporate.

3. Add in the stock with a cup of hot water and leave to cook for another 6-8 minutes. Add hot water if you need to.

4. Finally add the cream and let it simmer on a low heat for another 6-8 minutes. Serve hot with rice, baby potatoes, mash or bread.

6 SARDINES

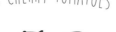

WHOLE & FRESH

8 CHERRY TOMATOES

CUT IN HALF

BABY SPINACH

1 LARGE HANDFUL

GARLIC

1 CLOVE, CRUSHED

BAGUETTE

CUT INTO SLICES

PARSLEY

1 HANDFUL, CHOPPED

OLIVE OIL

4 TABLESPOONS

FLOUR

FOR DUSTING

BUTTER

1 KNOB

GRILLED SARDINES
Served with Spinach, Cherry Tomatoes
and Garlic Bread

 SERVES 2

**"For some reason a lot of people are nervous about cooking
sardines yet they are so cheap and tasty. This recipe has
become one of our testers' favourites. Don't discount it until
you've tried it!"**

1. Pre-heat the oven to 180 degrees.

2. Heat 2 tablespoons of olive oil in a shallow pan on a medium
heat.

3. Season the sardines with a pinch of salt and pepper, dust with
some plain flour to prevent it from sticking to the pan, and fry
for 2 minutes on each side. Transfer to an oven dish and put in
the oven for 4-6 minutes.

4. While this is cooking mix the butter, garlic and parsley
together and spread on the sliced baguette. Put in the oven for
2-4 minutes.

5. Heat the remaining olive oil in a pan. Add the tomatoes and
spinach, seasoning with salt and pepper, and cook for 1 minute.
Placed the spinach on the plate then the sardines on top, with
the garlic bread on the side. Garnish with the parsley. Another
speedy show off meal.

SWEET TREATS

Cooking is fun, especially when you're experimenting with puddings and sweets. These easy and affordable desserts can be the perfect end to an evening meal, a tasty treat for a summer's afternoon, or the highlight of a children's birthday party – although we guarantee the grown-ups will enjoy them just as much as the kids.

COCONUT AND LIME SORBET

CASTOR SUGAR

250 GRAMS

COCONUT MILK

250ML CAN

1 LIME

JUICE AND ZEST

COCONUT AND LIME SORBET

 SERVES 4
(OR ONE PERSON NIGHT AFTER NIGHT)

"This is so quick and tasty that one of our colleagues ate it every night for four nights. Coconut milk can be expensive in the supermarket so if you use it a lot it may be worth looking out for it in an Asian grocery. In fact sometimes the supermarket sells less well known brands much cheaper in the 'world foods' section. Look out for it on the lower shelves – it tastes exactly the same!"

1. Mix all the ingredients together, put in a plastic container and freeze for 2 hours.

2. Take it out of the freezer, use a fork mix it up, and return to the freezer for further 1 ½ hours.

3. Take out and serve. YUM!

CARAMELISED APPLE AND PEAR UPSIDE DOWN CAKE

4 RIPE PEARS

CORED AND CUT INTO WEDGES

4 COOKING APPLES

OR GRANNY'S SMITHS –
CORED AND CUT INTO WEDGES

BUTTER

125 GRAMS UNSALTED

GROUND CINNAMON

2 TEASPOONS

4 LARGE EGGS

CASTER SUGAR

135 GRAMS

A PINCH OF NUTMEG

PLUS A PINCH
OF MIXED SPICES

SELF-RAISING FLOUR

225 GRAMS

BAKING POWDER

½ TEASPOON

CARAMELISED APPLE AND PEAR UPSIDE DOWN CAKE

 SERVES 4

1. You will need a 23cm square baking tin for this.

2. Preheat the oven to 180 degrees.

3. Heat a frying pan on a low heat. Add 35g of sugar and 2 tablespoons of water and cook gently until the sugar starts to caramelise. Add the apples and pears, sprinkle half of the spices over them, give them a gentle shake then leave to simmer for 4-6 minutes. Set to one side to cool.

4. In a deep large bowl, sift in the flour and baking powder then add the remaining spices. Mix well then add the remainder of the sugar, the butter and the eggs. Beat until combined.

5. Assemble the apples and pears in a cake tin, pour the mixture over them, and bake for 25-30 minutes. Turn upside down onto a cake plate and leave to cool. If you want to try some crumbs before it's cool be careful not to burn your fingers!

John's
Story

My parents were alcoholics who didn't take care of me and my siblings, and eventually there was a house fire that resulted in me being moved into care. I was moved around from house to house and I didn't enjoy it.

When I was 16 I started going to the bookies and this became an addiction for me – something I could enjoy. So I would go a lot, and eventually this was just where all my money went, the little I had. I never held down a stable job and although I never turned to drugs or alcohol, my gambling addiction crippled me financially and meant that I had nowhere solid to stay and ended up selling the Big Issue in the unpredictable Edinburgh weather.

One day Social Bite asked me if I'd like a job with them starting on the dishes. At first I just did a few hours a day, but now I'm working full time out at the central kitchen where all of our food and recipes are made. I make all of our homemade desserts and our famous carrot salad that accompanies the hot meals we serve in the shop. I'm also back together with my wife who I had been apart from for years, and we are living together in Portobello with our son and are much happier.

John Brown

12 DIGESTIVE BISCUITS

BUTTER

50 GRAMS MELTED

MASCARPONE SOFT CHEESE

300 GRAMS
(BUT THIS WOULD WORK WITH OTHER
SOFT CHEESE IF THAT'S WHAT YOU HAVE)

DOUBLE CREAM

150ML

ICING SUGAR

2 TEASPOONS

1 LEMON

JUICE AND ZEST

JOHN'S EMERGENCY CHEESE CAKE

31

SERVES 4
(OR A GREEDY TWO IN OUR CASE)

"Sometimes you just need cheese cake fast and this no cook version is our favourite. We like to make this in early summer when strawberries and raspberries are cheaper but you can also use frozen berries. It's also a good dish to serve when you want to impress someone and when you've made it once you can whip it up in no time."

1. Put the biscuits in a see through bag, then crush them using a rolling pin until crumbled.

2. Put the biscuit crumbs into a bowl, add the melted butter and mix well. Divide the biscuit mixture into 4 dessert glasses without pressing it down firmly. Put it in the fridge to cool.

3. Mix the mascarpone cheese, double cream, lemon juice and zest together in a mixing bowl until smooth. Be careful not to over mix as this will result in a thick mixture or it will split.

4. Spoon the mixture into the glasses just half way, then put them back in the fridge to set for about 20-25 minutes.

5. Top with fruit of your choice.

6. Meanwhile blend most of the fruit with the icing sugar using a food processor until smooth.

7. To serve, spoon the berry sauce over the cheese mixture, decorate with the remaining berries, dust with icing sugar and serve.

FOUR RIPE BANANAS

SELF-RAISING FLOUR

180 GRAMS

SUGAR

160 GRAMS

UNSALTED BUTTER

180 GRAMS

4 MEDIUM EGGS

CINNAMON

1/2 TEASPOON

NUTMEG

1/2 TEASPOON

KNOB OF BUTTER

BANANA CAKE

(32)

⊖ SERVES 2

"This is a really good way of using up bananas that are beginning to go past their best. It's also something that children enjoy making or helping with. It also works well with a melted Easter egg on top! You'll need an 18cm baking tin for this but once you've made it we promise you'll be making it again and again."

1. Pre-heat the oven to 160 degrees.

2. Peel the bananas and put them in a large bowl, then mash them using a fork.

3. Add the rest of the ingredients to the bowl and mix with an electric whisk (or a hand whisk and elbow grease) until smooth.

4. Grease the baking tin with a knob of butter. Pour in the mixture and bake for 45-55 minutes. Put a skewer through it to check that it is dry in the centre. If not put back in for another 5 minutes or so. Once it's cooked, let it cool then serve.

2 BANANAS

VANILLA ICE CREAM

4 SCOOPS

LIME JUICE

½ TABLESPOON

MILK

1 PINT

SUNNY DAY BANANA AND LIME MILKSHAKE

🍜 SERVES 2

"You can experiment with different fruits for this milkshake. Soft fruits like blueberries and strawberries work well. Frozen fruit is nice too, and there's no need to defrost. If you've bought too many bananas you can slice and freeze them so they are ready for the next time. Apparently this recipe is our publisher's favourite!"

I. Mix everything in a blender – you can use a stick blender for this.

2. Once it's fully blended, pour into large glasses and serve.

THREE MINUTE LEMON CURD
AND RICOTTA PANCAKE

6 READY-MADE CREPES

RICOTTA CHEESE

6 TABLESPOONS

LEMON CURD

6 TABLESPOONS

CASTER SUGAR

2 TEASPOONS

KNOB OF BUTTER

THREE MINUTE LEMON CURD AND RICOTTA PANCAKE

 SERVES 6
(BUT ONLY THREE IN PRACTICE)

"This is a real cheat dish but you won't hear any complaints and if you're feeling energetic you can always make your own crepes."

1. Preheat the oven to 170 degrees.

2. You don't have much to do for this dessert so whilst the oven is heating you could ring your mum, do some washing up or just tick something annoying off your to do list.

3. Spread the cheese on the pancakes, add the lemon curd, fold in half, put on the butter, sprinkle on some sugar, and put in the oven for about 2 minutes. Serve and enjoy!

ICE CREAM

ANY FLAVOUR
OF YOUR CHOICE

BISCUITS

LEFTOVER OF YOUR CHOICE
– WE THINK GINGER
BISCUITS ARE GOOD

KNOB OF BUTTER

AMELIA, RHIANNA & YANDAY'S ICE CREAM AND BISCUIT CRUMBLE

 SERVES 2

"Michael came up with this idea one evening when his daughters wanted ice cream with apple pie. Unfortunately there was no apple pie. He found some biscuits that were going soft, got the kids to help crumble them, put them in the oven and used them to top ice cream. Ever since then they've made it whenever they're having ice cream."

1. Pre-heat the oven to 180 degrees.

2. Crumble the leftover biscuits – children like to help with this part!

3. Put the crumbled biscuits on an oven tray, mix in the butter, then put them in the oven for about 2-4 minutes until crunchy.

4. Scoop the ice cream into a bowl, sprinkle the biscuit crumble on top, and serve. It's a winner!

Our Head Chef Michael's Story

I was the first employee of Social Bite, employed when Josh and Alice were doing finishing touches to the Rose Street Café in Edinburgh. I remember even popping in several times to help with little things like painting, cleaning floors and so on. I'd been offered another job at the time but this project was so inspiring that I wanted to be part of it.

I am originally from Sierra Leone but have lived in Kirkcaldy since 2003. Before that I was in London, where I worked for the Hilton Hotel as a Senior Chef De Partie.

Working for Social Bite is the best thing to ever happen to me, because it is very inspiring to work with the homeless guys. When the guys first get the opportunity to come and work beside me, they have no knowledge of how to even use a knife. Some of them have never even had a job and it's great to see them becoming more confident in their cooking. One guy was so nervous he was shaking when he held the knife but now he can get on with anything. Not only are these guys learning how to cook, they are making better lives for themselves and their families.

Social Bite is like a big family, of which I am extremely proud to be a part.

ACKNOWLEDGEMENTS

With thanks to Gary Callaghan, Tracy Rowan, Julie Lennox, Nic Rollo and Amanda Thomson; Helen Sedgwick, Gill Tasker and Simon Cree at Cargo; Kate MacLeary, Andrew Forteath, Kouki Gharra, Geraldine McMorrow, Davinder Samrai and Laurel Stevens at Freight.

NB: All food photography was taken by ordinary people with no background in catering (or professional photography!) who made recipes themselves.